Down and Out in New

Homeless

A Dishono

Down and Out in New York City

Homelessness:
A Dishonorable Poverty

Tony D. Guzewicz

Nova Science Publishers, Inc.

Art Director: Christopher Concannon
Graphics: Elenor Kallberg and Maria Ester Hawrys
Book Production: Michael Lyons, Roseann Pena,
                Casey Pfalzer, June Martino,
                Tammy Sauter, and Michelle Lalo
Circulation: Irene Kwartiroff, Annette Hellinger,
             and Benjamin Fung
Cover Design: Concannon

Library of Congress Cataloging-in-Publication Data

Guzewicz, Tony.
    Down and out in New York City : homelessness,
a dishonorable poverty / Tony Guzewicz.
        p. cm.
    Includes bibliographical references and index.
    ISBN 1-56072-159-6 : $24.95
    1. Homeless persons--New York (N.Y.)--Case studies.
I. Title.
HV4506.N7G88   1993   93-38458
362.5'09747'1--dc20   CIP

© 1994 Nova Science Publishers, Inc.
  6080 Jericho Turnpike, Suite 207
  Commack, New York 11725
  Tele. 516-499-3103 Fax 516-499-3146
  E Mail Novasci1@aol.com

Printed in the United States of America

Table of Contents

Acknowledgments

For my parents Rita and Tony Guzewicz. Most of all to my wife Krista for her
unfailing support and patience. And to my friend Jay Mancini.
I will always be grateful for their love and continuing belief in me.

My deepest gratitude extends to all those who allowed me to enter their lives.
My thoughts will always be with them.

Preface

In recent years increasing national attention has focused on the plight of homeless persons, many of whom are living on the streets of major cities. Although the problem of homelessness is an old one, this new awareness is a reflection of recent economic difficulties that have both increased the numbers and changed the traditional make-up of this population.

In New York City alone, this niche of American life has gone from 36,000 to 90,000. The number of people living in boxes and in doorways and pleading for money has grown, and so has a kind of tension for many who waiver between sympathy, anger and fear--as the face of poverty becomes a part of their daily lives.

Homelessness does not stem from any one cause, but results from a combination of factors--including the extreme poverty and alienation of individuals who live alone or are without family and are physically, mentally or socially disabled. The lack of jobs in a depressed economy, cutbacks in government welfare and social service programs, and a shortage of affordable housing are also contributing factors.

Many of us tend to lump all the homeless together into a single, faceless category. It's easy to see why. We seldom actually hear the voices of the homeless. When we see them on television or read about them in newspapers, the homeless often blur into a single group of poor, desperate people with little initiative and few aspirations. As a result, we lose sight of the fact the homelessness has many individual faces.

For many years, the stereotype of a homeless person was that of the single, white, male alcoholic--the "bum." Many of the homeless are, in fact, winos. And many of them are drug addicts. But growing numbers are not. The face of America's homeless now mirrors the face of America's poor.

Fearful people turn aside when they see a homeless person. Youths harass them, thieves rob them, psychopaths burn them. Only recently have they appeared in large enough numbers to enter the public consciousness as a group apart--part pity and part fear. The curious wonder who they are, how they became homeless, why they live on the streets, and if perhaps they themselves may one day become one of them. But for most people, the homeless remain as they have always been-- essentially invisible--most of them passing their days unseen by the rest of us.

Money. Too old, too sick or unskilled to work, many of the homeless are simply unable to amass the documents or otherwise negotiate the bewildering bureaucratic maze of appointments, application forms, interviews and follow-ups required of those who receive public assistance. As many of them know from experience, one lost document, one missed appointment, one wrong answer, their case can be closed making the very effort to comply seem futile.

It is often believed that people are homeless by choice, because of laziness or because they are unwilling to control their intake of drugs or alcohol. If homeless people are indeed responsible for their own plight, how does one explain the rapid increase particularly among women with dependent children? It's true that some of the homeless are former mental patients, but has the number of irresponsible or psychologically disturbed people really increased in recent years? Research clearly indicates that the bulk of deinstitutionalization took place in the earlier decades of the 1950s, 60s, and 70s, while the dramatic increase of homelessness did not begin until the early 1980s.

While housing has centered around the needs of the homeless, there is a need for a "support" type system which could help people adjust and make the transition from being homeless to returning to society. Their chances of regaining their lost economic and social status depends upon their physical and mental rehabilitation.

There were shelters twenty years ago and there are shelters today. However, with the drastic increase in homelessness, the availability of drugs, and the increase in crime in the shelter system, many of these people prefer to live on the streets where they feel safer. As one homeless person told me "shelters are like a chalk-line between death and hell. The guards beat on you, the people beat on each other. Disease is everywhere. I tried it once and couldn't take it."

A proportion of homeless persons need services which extend beyond that of temporary shelter. If such persons are to succeed in permanent housing, they need an opportunity to remain in a facility which will allow them, with professional assistance, to better cope and function within the realm of society. Support services for homeless persons must be designed by considering the various needs of these individuals.

The backgrounds and prior experiences of the homeless may include a number of problems apart from the lack of housing. Some may have experienced deinstitutionalization, others suffer alcohol and drug dependencies, while still others have experienced domestic violence or are school drop-outs. Every homeless person, regardless of their reason for homelessness, has experienced some degree of emotional distress brought about by the dislocation which extends the personal crisis of losing one's home.

These are people many of us would prefer not to know--"losers," people down on their luck. Call them what you wish. I could not escape from the fact that they are homeless and rootless, unwanted, very much alone and afraid.

No one is born into the existence depicted in this book. Those who think themselves immune from it, those who have homes and jobs now should know that Susan, Bobby and Jimmy, and every other person I know once had a home, a job and a family.

-----*Tony D. Guzewicz*
New York, 1993

Method

These are portraits of some of the people in New York City who are part of the homeless population. The methodology used in this book is ethnographic, to grasp the homeless point of view as accurately as possible: if you want to know what it's like to be homeless, you have to live it yourself. The countless days and nights I spent on the streets enabled me to put into practice what I had learned in preliminary conversations with homeless people.

I was concerned with the important questions of how people evolved into this situation and how if ever they got out. Once a person was without shelter, what strategies did he or she use to survive? Where did a person find food, go to the bathroom? Where did one sleep? Where did one shower or clean oneself? How were the hours of one's days filled?

Having established a casual acquaintance with these people, it became a matter of how to transform the superficial relationship into one of greater depth. At first I concentrated on keeping the atmosphere informal. Gaining their acceptance was always the first step, but gaining their trust was always a very difficult second step.

As a rule, I introduced myself as a photographer/writer and would not take photographs for quite some time. Usually, I carried a camera and micro cassette recorder and would record my impressions, any dialogue, or conversations for later transcribing. I tried to have the most vivid visual and narrative information possible, but I was not willing to violate the naturalness of the setting. The photographs are documents portraying the development of relationships that cover over five years. Sometimes I took few photographs and recorded little.

As I became more involved, I often left camera and recorder behind and was there as a friend, a listener. Though I never let anyone know where I lived, I did give them my phone number to call me if they needed something or if they just wanted someone to talk to. For me, the rights and desires of the people I became friends with were more important than a final purpose that would justify making images when they would not be welcomed.

The relationships I developed with these people is very complex. Dependent on the extent I was willing to give, whether I went home at night or whether I spent the night on the street, I often felt pulled into street life.

I remember one Christmas Eve I was walking on the Lower East Side
of Manhattan and noticed bodies bedded down under wet cardboard
on the sidewalk, others crouched, dejected in doorways, though the lucky one's
had plastic covering to protect themselves. The rest sat shivering. How easy
it could have been to walk past. How easy it could have been to sympathize from
a distance. How easy it could have been to walk on the other side of the street.
I stopped and stayed the night among some friends. As we talked a line from
George Orwell's Down and Out in Paris and London flashed through my mind
"here is the world that awaits you if you are ever penniless."

You can see something in the faces of the homeless--their sadness
and disappointment in having the "American dream" become their nightmare.
Their faces speak of a living hell on the streets of our cities,
of an existence they do not want.

These are the stories of the people I know--some who have made it,
and others I bade good-bye to in a bag. Through an approach that allows these
people to speak through my voice, it is hoped that they will no longer remain silent
and that all of us can have a clearer understanding of what it means
to be without a home.

It is with my discretion that the names of those people who appear
in this book have been changed.

VOICES

Linda--Age 22

Raised in a home, the youngest of three children, Linda's life was far from the "ideal American household." At the time, Linda was unaware that her father was an alcoholic and was abusing her mother. They never had time for her. Her brother and sister were much older and never had time for her either. Left alone most of the time, Linda craved love and attention which was never found. Little did she know at the time the role her family played in helping to shape her future.

At the age of ten, Linda's parents divorced and she and her mom moved from Michigan to Illinois. Trying to make ends meet, Linda's mom worked two jobs, day and night. Being a child of ten, with no one ever home, the only way Linda found attention was by getting into trouble.

While at school she enjoyed playing practical jokes on her teachers. Often her mom would punish her but she was never home and the punishment would go adrift. "When I was only thirteen and nobody was ever around, I had a lot of free time and it was easy to get into trouble." All her practical jokes were her way of getting attention at school.

By the time Linda was fourteen, she had been suspended from school over a dozen times. It was decided by the school and her mom that she would be sent to Applewood School for girls, which is a reformatory in Illinois. Linda never liked authority. She took an immediate disliking to Applewood because of its tough disciplinary standards. As time passed though, she grew to enjoy her stay there. For the first time in years she was given affection and felt cared for. Her stay lasted for one and a half years.

One day after she returned home from Applewood, she took her dog for a walk. She met a guy and they immediately hit it off. She quickly quit school and spent all her time with him. Several times her mom voiced her disapproval but let Linda do what she wanted. Her boyfriend flowered her with more love and affection than she ever thought possible. About a year later, they were married, already with one child and was pregnant with their second. She was one of the happiest women alive as her life began to have meaning.

A few months after her marriage, her mother passed away. Things started to fall apart rapidly. Her husband would start beating her for no apparent reason. "At first I thought I'd done something wrong. I couldn't understand why he'd beat

me up for no reason. I tried to talk to him and he'd say I needed to be disciplined.
He'd tell me he loved me. I didn't leave because I was scared and depressed
and I was afraid to be on my own again." What made matters worse for Linda
was that her husband's family was in the syndicate. He allowed her no friends
and no phone. If he went out, he'd lock her in the apartment from the outside,
or he'd have his cousins watch over her. "I felt like I was a prisoner
in my own home."

The next three years were to be the worst years of Linda's life. After her parents divorce, she had lost contact with her father, brother and sister. Her husband would often go into violent rages. "One minute everything was fine and the next minute he'd turn around and beat the hell out of me." He'd beat her because she was "bad" and wouldn't do as she was told.
"If I was told to do something I'd get rebellious."

Often while she was asleep her husband would handcuff her to the bed. Sometimes she'd be cuffed for two days at a time. "One time I had to go to the bathroom so bad and he wouldn't uncuff me. I wound up going right on the bed." He'd constantly go on binges beating her, hitting her with broom sticks, kicking her down stairs. There were times she needed medical attention but her husband wouldn't take her to a hospital for treatment.

As time passed, the situation grew progressively worse. "I remember one time I was asleep and he handcuffed me to the bed. He went out and when he returned, he was with five of his friends. He sat in a chair next to the bed and watched as his friends came in one by one and raped me. When they finished, he left me cuffed and I just cried for a long time."

One time Linda answered her husband back. "He tied me up and took a hot iron and kept putting it on different parts of my body. He gagged me so I couldn't scream. I knew he'd have killed me if I said anything." On another occasion, he played Russian roulette. "He showed me a gun and every other chamber had a bullet in it. I prayed. I was really scared that I was going to die. After he pulled the gun on me I lost feeling for everything. I could have died and it would have been no big deal. In a way I wanted to die but I wasn't able to commit suicide. I was hoping in a way that he'd do it. I didn't want to live and I couldn't kill myself. I was afraid to leave and I was confused and very depressed." Usually, when he beat or tortured her, the kids were at his cousin's house next door. They were very young and never knew what was going on. He would never touch her in front of the children.

Sometimes her husband would tell her that he was going to change and she would want him to go for counseling. She'd think that things would return to normal, the way they used to be. When this happened, she would have a glimmer of hope which always quickly dissolved.

She recalls the worst experience of her life. "We had just made love and I thought everything was fine. He told me to sit in a chair. Then he handcuffed and gagged me, and put a clock on a table that was beside the chair. He told me "in forty-five minutes you're going to die." I just went numb. I was scared to death.

When the alarm went off, he pulled the trigger but the gun wasn't loaded. In a way I was hoping he would kill me so I wouldn't have to go through this anymore."

A few months before Linda "escaped" she got a pit bull. "It was great. I trained the dog. He hated my husband. If he tried to hurt me, the dog would attack him." One day her husband decided to take the dog for a walk which he had never done before. "I knew he probably went to kill the dog and when he came back, he was probably going to kill me. I found some money and without thinking I ran out of the house to the train station. I had to leave my kids because I didn't have enough money to take them with me. It was them or me."

She came to New York in sheer desperation. She knew her husband wouldn't look for her here because she hates big cities. She arrived with just the clothes on her back and two dollars in her pocket. "All I thought about was that I got away. I finally did it. Now I understand why women don't leave men who abuse them. There is a lot of fear--fear of being found and possibly killed."

When she talked about her future she said "I'd like to have a few friends, a job and get myself straightened out. I haven't seen my kids in a while. I ache for them constantly. At the same time, I feel exhilarated because I got away. Because now I have a chance. I am going to make it, but I still wonder if I have any worth."

Shortly after her ordeal, with the help of some friends, Linda was placed into a shelter for battered women where she has been under care. Because of the strict policies of the shelter, I've been unable to keep in touch with her.

Kalif and Cascadus--Mid 40s

On Ninth Street and Avenue C there is a group of homeless people trying
to restore a sense of community to thee homeless of New York.
Kalif and Cascadus came to New York with the intention of doing something
positive about homelessness. Using donated and discarded material they set up
an outdoor kitchen and constructed teepees for themselves and others to live in.
Neighborhood support has been great. As people quickly learned about their
project, both homeless and non-homeless people offered support in the way
of donations--money, energy and time. At any time of the day or night,
the encampment is active with people working,
visiting or just coming to meet and talk.

"We started out serving a few people a day. Now we estimate that we
serve about three hundred." Originally, food started being served at 3:00
in the afternoon and ended at 10:00 but the need has been greater than that.
They'd like to provide food 24 hours a day. They operate on donations and can
always use more food, volunteers, kitchen supplies. There is no government

support--this is people doing for each other. "We figure that it costs about 10
cents a meal to serve people here." All of the homeless here agree that the food
is much better than that of city shelters and the atmosphere is not dangerous,
as the shelter atmosphere often is." Everyone helps with cleaning up or some
aspect of preparation and no one is asked to make a donation
if he or she has no money.

The "Temple of the Rainbow" kitchen is joined with the neighborhood
in fighting the impending gentrification of the area. Already, the "Christadora
House" condominium development looms over the area, where studio apartments
were advertised for $120,000. Kalif and Cascadus note that the neighborhood
has appreciated the positive effects of the kitchen. "Everyday, even the police,
have said that crime is down. If someone's got a meal in his stomach
he's not as inclined to steal for food or to feel angry and frustrated.
Drugs and violence aren't allowed here, otherwise everyone is welcome."

Jimmy--Age 25

"I never thought that I'd be homeless, but my building went co-op and I couldn't afford my apartment anymore. One day I had a job and an apartment, and the next...living on the street looking up at the building I used to live in." Jimmy, became an active member of the Temple of the Rainbow kitchen shortly after he became homeless. "I lost my apartment and then I lost my job. I started hanging out on the corner with the other guys, getting drunk, panhandling, waking up on the street with a hangover and getting drunk again. I realized that I didn't want to get into that kind of lifestyle." He heard about the kitchen and came down here where he met his girlfriend and has been helping out since.

"We are fixing up an abandoned building with some other people. They all have the same problem--finding an affordable apartment in New York. We're working on cleaning the place out. We don't want to live here forever, but at least it's a place for now, until we can get back on our feet."

"Sure it's a pain not being able to take a shower but there is a hydrant across the street. The people here are strong supporters of squatters rights. They've fought to keep the place we're staying in. If we hear of anyone having an eviction problem, we get a group together to go to that building and organize a protest."

Jimmy's squat is on a block on which half of the buildings are abandoned. Often, these are city owned buildings which were seized due to unpaid taxes or buildings that an owner chose to abandon because, at the time, they were in an undesirable section of town. Most abandoned buildings generate some kind of activity. Some become "crack houses," others become residences for those who cannot afford housing. People who squat find that the only time attention is paid to these buildings is when an area is redeveloped and they are forced out by developers.

Squatting is a challenge. Without a flashlight, the building is pitch dark. The floor is unsteady, cluttered with fallen beams and other signs of neglect. While fixing the building Jimmy stays in he fell through the stairway that he was trying to fix. He did damage to his back and ankle, unable to work on the building anymore.

"Anyone could be is this situation. The only difference between you and us is that right now you have a job and an apartment."

What are they going to do? The city gets down on homeless people but they make their own problems with rents. It wasn't like this before. When I was a kid growing up here, I didn't see all these big lines of people at soup kitchens--people corner to corner panhandling. It wasn't here.

How loud is my voice is this society? Look at the level I'm on and the level that they're on.

You might see someone lying on the street drunk but you've
got to remember that he's still a person.

Bobby--Age 38

"I called my parents in Brooklyn today. When my father found out that my mother was talking to me, he hung up the phone." Bobby, who hasn't gotten along with his parents since he was sixteen told me how the kids in his family were a little wild. They were into drugs like pot and LSD. However, he did get along well with his sisters but has since lost contact with them.

Bobby, who's had a history of alcoholism, used to work for a major New York newspaper. During the first few years of employment his drinking went unnoticed. However, it progressively worsened as he began drinking at work and was given warnings from fellow workers. Eventually he was terminated because he started drinking heavily. At the time he was living on Eighth Street and Avenue B in a rent stabilized apartment. His landlord offered him $4,000 to leave which he quickly accepted. He began hanging out with friends and spent the money he received on supporting his dependency without realizing the consequences. Bobby never thought that he wouldn't be able to find another place to live.

"It's hard to stop drinking on the street, and when you go to detox you only stay there three to five days. I was even turned down from detox once because I wasn't drunk enough. When you come out you have no place to go back to except the streets. Then I get the shakes and I need alcohol like I need medicine."

He's been in this neighborhood for some time and is known by the people who live here. People know him and sometimes even bring him some food. "One guy comes by every week and brings me breakfast. Some of the people around here talk to me, give me old clothes and food."

"I don't want anything from the government anymore. The city has a turnstile system. Bring them in, drug them up, and throw them out. Round and round. That's the city's thing. In a word the sweep up of the homeless sucks. It's unconstitutional. If people want to stay on the street rather than go to a shelter they should have the right to. If you're not already crazy, the city will make you crazy."

Bobby spends much of his time reading. However, he doesn't get as much time to read as he'd like because it's very hard to hold onto anything in the street. He told me that he'd like to read The Brothers Karamazov by Dostoyevsky again because he can identify with Dimitri who was an alcoholic too.

I know that a person can be up today and tomorrow may not know where they're going or where they're going to get they're next mouthful of food. You really feel it sometimes when people come by and see you on the street and put you into the same category. If you look like you're not in the same position as they are, you're nobody, nothing.

Bobby, once involved with a woman told me of a son he has down south. "If I could get him back things would change. I'd work at cutting out my drinking. I'd have something to work for."

I came here about three and a half years ago. I was a heavy junky back home in Malaysia. On dope all the time for twelve years.

One of my friends was an entertainer. He came to New York and said I could make good money in nightclubs. My family thought a change of environment would do me good so they got the money together and sent me. They thought I might be able to straighten out here. Here I am thirty-three years old and I got nothing.

When I first got to New York I got a job in a Chinese nightclub. I started work on Christmas Eve. I was making over $100 in tips every night. I worked there four or five months, working from 9:00 at night until 4:00 in the morning, seven days a week. I started drinking at work because I wasn't on dope anymore. It probably cost me my job because I was half drunk by the end of the night.

There were some guys in the nightclub that I used to hang around with. They were a kind of street gang. All we did was fight, eat, get high, freebase or snort coke. I was with them for about a year and then, one day, because of a girl, they wanted to fuck me up so I left. Before I left I made a score with some dope-- about $7,000. I thought of going back home but I fucked it up on freebase. All $7,000 in two weeks.

I've been hanging around the streets now for about two years. I got no money so what can I do? I hang around with old guys, all kinds of people but mostly alcoholics. They taught me how to panhandle, so I started panhandling. I've been sleeping on the street winter, summer, all year round. I sleep in the park on benches, on the trains, hallways, anywhere I can find a quiet and safe place. I need a job but what can I do? I'm not experienced in anything and legally I'm not a citizen.

I got my reasons for not being in touch with my family. If I contact them and say I'm working, they'll want me to send back money. My parents are old and also I don't want to hear that my mom or dad passed away or something. So I feel bad and they probably feel bad. It's better for me not to have contact with them. I miss them too. I dream about them, I think about them every day. Even if I wanted to go back home I'd have to go with money because I have to pay them back for sending me here.

My family is more eastern thinking than me. They're more traditional. We don't understand each other. I want to be free and be left alone to do what I want. It's a much different kind of life in Malaysia. That's why I get fed up with life and start drinking, shooting coke, and smoking crack. It's not an excuse. I'm just tired and I want to fuck myself up. What else is there to live for? I can't get a place to live, I can't get a job. So you take away my dignity and self-respect and what do I have left? My only consolation of the day is to go and get high. That's all I have.

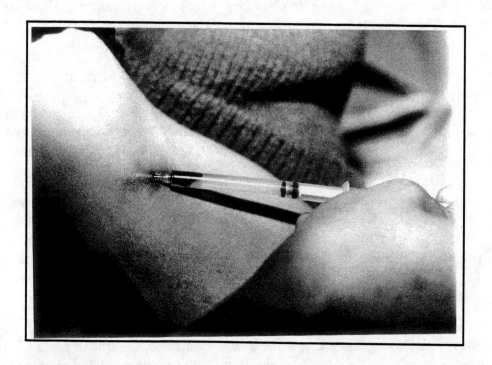

You know what my parents used to do to me so I couldn't get high? They'd put me in a room and put a chain around my leg and the bed so I couldn't move and then they'd lock the door too. They only let me out to eat dinner and take a shower and then they would chain me up again. I never got busted for dope. It was my family who used to turn me in all the time. Dope was very easy to get back home and all my friends were on it. I guess that's why I came to America, to try and do something because I was tired of it all. I was on it for twelve years, and every time I tried to quit cold turkey I'd go back to it. I don't know why but probably because I was stupid.

It's common to see a wino with his wine bottle and guys passed out
on the street. What you don't see is the other addiction--drug addiction.
It's a shame that so much attention is paid to alcohol because it's a national drug.
It's legal to use. Most people don't bring their addiction to the street--the street
causes it. They figure what the fuck, I'll probably die before I'm fifty so I might
as well be the least miserable that I can. The only way is through cheap wine
or drugs which are cheaper in New York. You don't see the addict as often
and you don't see him suffer as much. I've had an alcohol problem as well
but drugs entail a lot more in terms of suffering. Believe me, I know.

Life is so boring and miserable. I hang around with my alcoholic friends
and sometimes they get so fucked up that I get fed up with them. I don't want
to hang around with them but they're the only friends I got. Where can I go?
So I turn to drugs. I mean life is so miserable in New York City.
The government don't do shit, they don't help you with shit, nothing.

I make some money every day but what can I do? What am I gonna do with
the money? Just enough to eat and drink, that's all. I can't afford an apartment.
I go look for a job and they look at me and say I'm dirty and I gotta clean myself
up. Where am I gonna clean myself up. I went to a shelter one time and there was
a man who had a watch. These other guys wanted it and went up to him and just
kept beating him and finally took it off his hand. I won't go there anymore.

During the summer I was sleeping next to a newsstand and these guys came
up to me and started beating on me. One guy hit me with a lead pipe and I ended
up at the hospital. Another time I was sitting on the side of a restaurant
on the corner where I always sit. The owner came out and said to get out of here.
When he hit me in the face I thought he just used his fist.
But when he walked away I saw that he had a club.

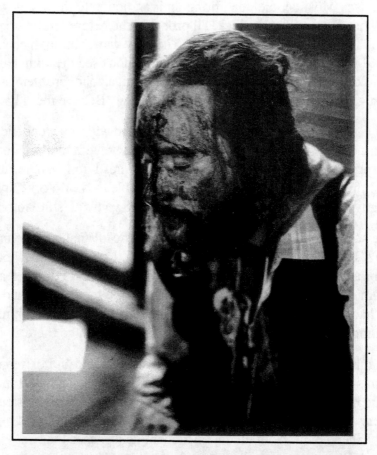

One night while Pat was sleeping he was severely beaten and stabbed.
By the time his body was discovered, it was too late. Pat lie dead, his misery finally over.

Ann--Age 67

I'm sixty-seven years old. I've been living on the streets for the past eight years after my husband died. They (the Social Security) don't give me enough money to get a place to live. People have told me to go the suburbs or to a state where things are cheaper. I've been all over and, believe you me, the rents are high everywhere. When they know you don't have much money up front, they (landlords) won't take you for an apartment.

I'd like to have a place to live because I like to do my own cooking, and I wouldn't have to stand in line for my food. This is everything I own. Now my home has been where I plop myself.

When I had a home, I used to do all kinds of charity work. I'd collect for the Cancer Society, Muscular Dystrophy. I started taking a class about poor people and one of my neighbors asked me what I was doing. Of course, at the time, I had no idea that I would be poor one day. Then my neighbor started taking the class and said she didn't know that there were so many poor people in this country. I told her the Lord has blessed me. I have a husband and a home. I'd like to give something back to those who don't have. I had no idea that I would ever end up homeless.

I have arthritis, high blood pressure and an ulcer. There are days when I wake up and say gee whiz, nothing hurts today. But those days are rare. I have a hard time standing in line for things, going up and down stairs. Usually I just sit in the park all day. At night and on weekends I stay in the alcove in front of the bank, after it closes. I get a warm breeze from the subway entrance and I've got some protection from the wind and rain. The difficult thing about being here is that it's hard to find a bathroom. The nearest public bathroom is in the park and that's too far for me to walk with all my things. There's a young man who sleeps in the corner here who will sometimes watch my things for me.

I don't go to shelters anymore. It's not worth it. One time I went to a women's shelter and got undressed and got into bed. I left my clothes all folded up on a chair next to me. Pants, underwear, shoes. When I woke up the next morning, everything was gone. No one would admit to taking it. They gave me a thin house dress, a pair of slippers--the kind you wear in a hospital, and a token. That's what I had to go back to the street with.

Nowadays, they've got condominiums everywhere, even in Brooklyn.
They're very nice but they would never fix up a building like that for the homeless.
They wouldn't make as much money on it. It's hard to get a low rent and when
the landlord knows you don't have much money,
they really don't want you to live there.

This woman with furs and jewelry all over her came up to me and said
that she'd seen me on the street here for three years and I always look content.
She told me that her life was unhappy, how can I look so content with myself.
I told her that I was happy with who I was. There's no sense getting upset
about a situation that you can't do anything about.

I've been out here about eight years now. My husband and I owned a jewelry store. We were in a car accident. He was killed and I was in the hospital for weeks. We didn't have the license number of the car that hit us so the police couldn't do anything. I lost everything paying hospital bills. My parents are both dead and I don't see much of the rest of my family, so I had nowhere else to go. I tried to stay in shelters, but every time I tried to save a little money it got stolen.

I've tried to look for a job but it's hard to get hired at my age. I lost my teeth in the accident and that doesn't help on a job interview. I mean, who wants to hire someone who has no teeth. It doesn't make a good impression.
Now I'm doing this--begging for money on the street.

I've called Victim Services but they said it will be a while before they can do anything. I have to go to welfare again to see if I can get some help, but that takes a long time too. You can't push them too hard. If you do, they say why do you think that you're more important than anyone else.

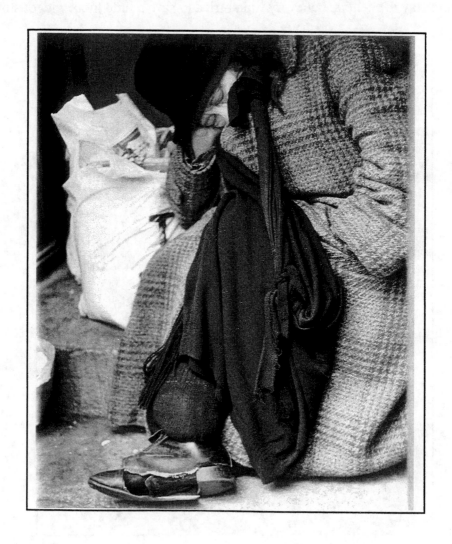

Ed--Age 32

I've been working since I was a teenager. Paid my taxes, social security.
One weekend I was playing hockey with some friends and I was in an accident.
I ended up in the hospital with a back injury and now
I have permanent nerve damage.

When I got out of the hospital, I couldn't go back to the job I was doing
because it was a physical job. My boss said he was sorry, but he didn't have
another job that he could give me. I had a three bedroom apartment in Brooklyn.
I was paying $200 a month. They were dying to get me out. Boy, every time
I was one day, two days late with the rent, I'd get an eviction notice in the mail.
When I was in the hospital, they did it. The marshals came in, changed the locks
on my doors and that was it. Now the landlord's getting
$1,000 a month for the same apartment.

When you're young, you're stupid. I didn't have any insurance and I didn't
have anything saved. You don't think anything's going to happen to you.
I went to Social Security about getting benefits and they told me that it may take
up to a year to get them. In the meantime, I'm out on the street.

I've been sleeping in the park with a couple of guys who watch out for each
other. I panhandle enough money to survive. You know what I've found?
People that don't have, that's who gives me money. The Wall Street types,
jumping in and out of their fancy cars--think they give me a dime?
No, they look at me like they're going to spit at me. It's the average people,
the people who can't spare it, that helps me out.

I was sleeping in the park a few nights ago and some kids came up to me and started beating on me with a baseball bat for no reason. I was trying to get away from them but they hit me on my arms and legs, all over. Then they just walked away laughing.

I don't like to sleep in the park--too many cuckoos. I have to sleep with one eye open. I usually sleep on the steps of A.A. for a while and then I walk around most of the night.

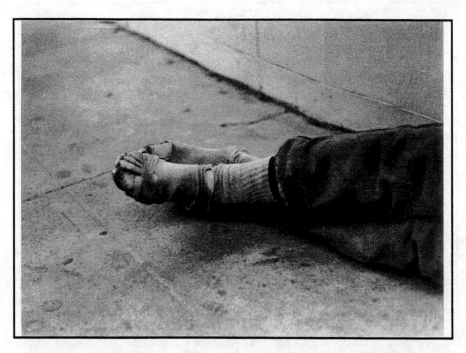

People will steal anything. Do you know that I woke up in the morning
on Ninth Street and somebody had even stolen the shoes off my feet.

Julian--Age 58

I've worked for over forty years, but now I'm fifty-eight and disabled. I get about $400 a month but what can I get with that? All of the apartments around here are about $800. I've been squatting in an abandoned building for a few years but I have to find another place to go. It's hard with my dog. A lot of people don't want dogs around. Even some of the squatters don't want them in the building. I've found that people who like dogs have good character. If you love animals, a dog can make your life so much happier.

The other day a man became very belligerent with me. He had the audacity to say that my dog was vicious and had tried to bite him. My dog doesn't bother anyone, but if he sees someone try to hurt me, he'll try to defend me. At about 11:00 every night I go to a dumpster near the butcher. They throw out meat and I know to go there every night. I used to go to a restaurant when they were closing and the manager decided that he wanted to take food home for himself so he told me "sorry, I can't give this to you anymore." Now I eat out of the garbage. That would probably kill most people--they wouldn't be able to handle it.

There was this guy with his little girl panhandling and he asked me for a cigarette. I said sure because I had a whole pack. Then he said "would you believe that I just stopped a lady. She had a whole pack and she wouldn't give me a cigarette." I said that I believed that. He said "I don't. I just lost my job and I have to panhandle now. I just can't believe these people." I asked him if, when he was working, and people asked him for a cigarette or change, would he help them out? He told me that he wouldn't. I told him that if he keeps hanging around here and he keeps panhandling till he gets a job, and he asks himself why? Remember when you had a job and you wouldn't help anybody.

Susan

I've been out here for nine years. I could write a book myself with
everything I've seen. When I get off the street,
I'm going to start writing things down.

I remember when I was a little girl that my father was a drinker.
I grew up in a small town down south. On Saturday nights my family would
have their banjo pickin', pig pickin' drinking, and they'd always give me beer.
I was about five years old. They'd think it was cute. They'd say, look she's
getting drunk. Well, by the time I was eighteen, I was an alcoholic.

The town I grew up in was so small that we all went to the same school.
By the time I was an adult, I had dated every guy my age in the whole town.
That's why I wanted to get out of that damn town.
Everyone knows your business.

Then I met the man who brought me to New York. The first man I met
in my life that was a con. He was on the streets and I didn't believe that anyone
should be on the streets--can you believe that. He was a drunk too.
Well, he became my partner, and then he became my old man, and then we came
to New York. We were living on the West Side and he was killed--stabbed.
I don't know who did it or why. I had to stay in New York for a year because
of the investigation and I went on a drunk.

When I first found out I was going to be homeless, this is when
the gentleman that brought me here died, it dawned on me that I was here
by myself. Scared. You're damn right I was scared. I had never lived
on the streets in my whole damn life. I thought about suicide, but then a bottle
of wine kept me going. "If anybody's on the street and they're not an alcoholic,
something's seriously wrong. Because nobody can stay on the street
and be either absolutely sane or not an alcoholic."

I went back home after that ordeal and stayed home for about a year.
I have two little girls at home who live with my mother. I had a hard time living
up to my family's expectations. My mom's sweet but I couldn't
be as "lady-like" as she wanted me to be.

I came back to New York with a girlfriend. It was supposed to be just
for the weekend. I got here, lost my car, and ended up on the street again.
I was staying with my uncle for a while but he died and I couldn't keep
the apartment, so I ended up on the street.

At first, New York was a winos paradise for me. I remember someone
handed me a joint--right on the street! I had never even seen a joint in my life.
I could get wine at all times of the day. I know now that alcoholism
is an illness and I have that illness.

I couldn't stay by myself and stay sober because I was too scared.
I started hanging out with the guys. They watched out for me. I was going
to A.A. weekly and the people there didn't always understand. They would say
that they saw me hanging out on the street with some bums. How could I do that.
I'd tell them that I was a homeless woman and that those guys watched out for me.
Were any of you willing to come out and stay with me on the street?

I thank the Lord though. I've been a lucky lady on the street. I've only been
raped once. That was by someone I thought I could trust. Well, he got paid back
and I'm thankful that I've stayed alive.

About four years ago I met my husband. He was on the street too.
He's getting an SSI check but it's only $400 a month. What the hell can you
do with $400? Section Eight housing is a joke. Welfare wouldn't give us a list
of apartments that would accept Section Eight. Did you ever try to find a landlord
who would accept welfare checks? We did find an apartment for a while that was
in such bad shape that we had to leave. We were always being robbed.
One day, someone smashed in the door and took everything we owned, right
down to underwear. We decided to look someplace else.

We asked to go to a family shelter. We were told that a married couple
was not considered a family. They wanted us to go to separate shelters.
We fought on this one. We got into this family shelter. You should have seen
it--no privacy. On the bed next to us, here's a lady smokin' dope with her little boy
watching t.v.. And over here we have a guy who's pimping the women in the place
and they're fighting over him. We didn't stay the whole night.
I'd rather stay on the street.

When we saved a little money, we were getting a hotel room two, maybe
three nights a week. We could take a bath, watch t.v.. It was a privilege to feel
normal. We're trying to save money now--send it back to my mother to keep
for us so we can't do that as much.

I remember a friend once took me to see a man about low income housing
for the homeless. I went to her place, took a shower and put on clean clothes.
Do you know what the man said to my friend? "She doesn't look homeless.
She's not dirty enough. I have a hard time believing that she needs housing as
much as someone else." I told him what the hell am I supposed to do.
If I'm drunk and dirty I'm not helping myself try to improve and I can't get any
help. Even when I was panhandling. If I was clean and sober no one would give
me money. But if I was drunk and lying on the street, I'd get money all the time.

People wonder why do we go to detox and then come back to the street
and drink. When you get out of detox and you're back on the streets with nowhere
to go, and you see what the city is like, why wouldn't you drink? You think you'll
have just one but it doesn't work. New York is like one big insane asylum
and I've got to get out of here before I find out where I fit in.

One night two of us were sleeping and I woke up because I felt warm.
I wasn't sure why and then I sat up and saw flames. At first, I thought that one
of us had left a cigarette burning but I saw crumpled up newspapers on fire all
around us. I couldn't believe it. Someone had set us on fire. They had put
newspaper and lighter fluid on top of us and lit it. The police said they'll try
and find the people but they have no idea as to who did it.
And we're the ones who are supposed to be crazy.

Robbie

You know, I have always considered myself to be a patriotic American but,
I'll tell you, this country is going to turn me into a socialist. At least socialist
countries give people a place to live and a job. That's got to be better than living
on the streets because you can't find a job that pays you enough money
to get a place to live.

Becoming homeless happens all at once. I had a nervous breakdown several
years ago and was hospitalized. I was married at the time and the doctors told my
wife that I would never recover. While I was under care she divorced me.
A few months later I was out of the hospital with nowhere to go. The hospital
told me to go to a flophouse that was nothing more than a shooting gallery.

I told them they were crazy, that I'd rather live on the streets than live like that. I remember thinking what am I going to do now? I didn't have that much money left. I went to an all night movie theater in Times Square and just sat there.

I went to one shelter where they didn't even have cots. You had to bring cardboard and sleep on the floor. People would walk around all night stealing. People were doing all kinds of drugs--I decided to leave.

I don't like to drink that much. I don't do any drugs except for an occasional joint. When my wife goes on a drunk I'm the one who's straight and can watch out for her, and try to get her to come off it. It's not always easy. Sometimes I know I just have to sit it out and wait for her to go through it. Then I make sure she gets to A.A.. When I go to the hospital for check-ups, the doctors look at my record and tell her that I'm a paranoid schizophrenic and that she should think twice about staying with me. She's told them that she accepts me with my illness and I accept her with hers.

We want to go back down south to live near my wife's family now. We've been saving money and sending it to her mother to put away for us. I've got to get out of this city. It's getting worse everyday. We can't even find a place to clean up anymore. All the public baths have closed down. During the summer, we've been going to the public pool and trying to use the showers there. You've got to be quick though. If the people there think that you're homeless and are using it as a public bath, they throw you out.

Do you know what it's like to try to find an apartment after you've been on the streets? I tried to go to the Bronx at one time. I gave the landlord money-- $1,500 in cash. We looked at the place. It was worth $400 a month. It would have taken all of my income (social security), but I thought that I could get an off-the-books job to make some extra money. So, I don't like to lie--I put down a mailing address (a shelter). The landlord said "oh no, not with that address." He found out where I was getting my income and said no. They want you to have a high-paying job so that they can raise the rent, whatever. He gave me back the money.

Currently, Susan and Robbie are off the street and are back down south. Susan is a recovering alcoholic and practicing registered nurse, while Robbie is a refrigeration/air conditioning repairman. We remain in contact by phone.

These guys are homeless. They have families, but families that are out of town that want no part of their lives. They don't go to shelters whether it's raining or freezing cold. They'll go to a movie and sit up all night. They'll take turns watching over each other. They're not related but will do anything for each other.

"We met on the street seven years ago and now we're closer than brothers. We'll do anything for each other, and when we get off the street, we'll leave together. People have to stick together on the street."

Jim

I used to play minor league baseball when I was younger. I even had a good shot at the major league. I wanted to play on the Boston Red Sox because I'm from Boston.

I went to Viet Nam, got into drugs, and couldn't get back into baseball. I was depressed because baseball was my life before I went to Nam and now

I couldn't get off drugs. I couldn't get on a methadone maintenance program
in Boston so I came to New York where I thought it would be easier. I've been
on maintenance now for a long time. Every time my dosage is lowered, I get really
sick and then they increase my dosage again. I've tried to stop but I've been
on it so long now that I don't think I can. I've been up and down so many times.

I keep dreaming that someday I'll get back into baseball. One weekend a guy
that comes around here brought us two baseball gloves and a ball.
Al sat up against the wall and I pitched to him. It felt good to hold that ball.
A few days later though, the gloves were stolen.
It's really hard to keep anything on the street.

Al

I've been in trouble in my lifetime. I spent a few years in prison for robbery--
I fucked up. My wife, she was a good woman but her family didn't approve
because I had been in trouble with the law. We've been divorced for a long time.

I really miss my kids. They're my pride and joy. My family knows where
they are but they won't talk to me so I can't get their addresses. My son, he's
about twenty-two and I think he lives in Florida. My daughter is around eighteen
now. I thought I saw her walk by the other day but I wasn't sure.

A few years ago I was sleeping in an abandoned building and the mattress I was sleeping on caught fire. My leg got burned badly. I ended up with gangrene and had to have my leg amputated. Now I need crutches to get around but it's hard to hold onto them. Do you believe that people actually steal them.
Once I was stuck in a doorway for two days because somebody stole them. The other night when I was sleeping somebody stole the bolts out of them--probably so I would fall when I got up.

I have a sister in Queens but she wants nothing to do with me. She works at a big insurance company in midtown. One day I went up to see her.
As soon as I got into the building and told the girl at the desk that I wanted to see my sister, the guard made me leave. She called the desk and told them to get rid of me. At least I have Jim--he's my family now.

Jose--Age 38

Things got bad for me after my wife died. We were living in Jersey City and I was driving a truck for a living. My wife was killed in a car accident. We had two kids who are with my sister now.
They don't know I'm on the street though.

I started to get into dope but I got hepatitis and now I won't have anything to do with it, cause I'm still not feeling good. There's no future in it. When you really look at it you really don't have no true, true friends out here. I don't sleep much either. The other guys call me "Johnny walker" because I just walk around all night. I stopped sleeping in the park because it's too dangerous.

My family's back in Puerto Rico but I want to get myself back together before I go there. I miss them--Christmas, New Years. Holidays used to mean something to me when I had them around. Now, a day like Christmas is just another day to me.

One night I was walking down a street and I put my head down because
it was raining. There was nothing coming but this truck came from nowhere
and nailed me. I was lying there bleeding and when I opened my eyes all I
remembered seeing was the tire. It was scary. I was in the hospital with all this
fluid in my lungs and one night I could hardly breathe. I thought
I was going to die in my sleep.

When I finally got discharged, I couldn't even walk. It was on a Saturday.
My clothes were all full of blood and they had cut my sweater open. I had to put
these same clothes on when I left the hospital. I was in so much pain that I had
to get drunk. The next day I ended up in a train station because I had nowhere
to go. I couldn't even get up. I hobbled all the way to the V.A.
and they admitted me and kept me for about a week.

I've been watching and listening and thinking to myself. Being on the streets
is a scary feeling. People I know out here have died and they say "you know
who died yesterday. He was alright." And the next day they don't even remember
who he was. I'm waiting to get healed now.

I have a lawyer and he says I have a case but it will take a while before
I see any money. Then I want to go back home to Puerto Rico
away from all this shit.

After nearly two years Jose received some money from his accident
and returned to his family.

My mother died when I was nine and my father died when I was twelve. I was sent to my aunt's in Cleveland and they didn't want me there, so I was sent back to New York when I was thirteen with nowhere to go.

I slept in hallways until I learned to steal. When I was old enough I put a gun in my hand. I've pimped, sold all kinds of drugs, and wound up getting busted during an armed robbery. At the time it was a matter of survival. People on the street sometimes do things they don't like to do but they have to in order to survive.

I spent five years in prison and all I want now is for society to open its doors so I can stick my feet in. Society should sit down and observe. Open its eyes and start caring and not turn its back on us. People don't care if you live or die. If they would stop and see how people on the street really are, they'd see for themselves that we're not crazy. People don't want to listen to us. I'm angry about what the city says it's doing for the homeless. The mayor should come out here and try it himself.

I did some tile work at a gym and I said to myself that I'll work hard to get
it finished quicker. It took me three weeks to do the bathroom, the floor,
the shower and the steam room. And the guy was only paying me $4.00 an hour--
seven days a week. After the work was finished, he led me to believe that he was
going to give me a job, but he didn't. Another guy that works for him came
by and saw me panhandling and told me that he'd try to help me, but that was
a while ago. I know that people have gone in there and asked who did the tile
work but I'd bet that my name wasn't even mentioned.

Everybody stops but nobody gives. I try to survive as best as I can.
Sometimes I don't have enough money to get a sandwich. I can't go
to the supermarket cause I don't have enough money. I do the best I can,
that's all I can say. I'm a scavenger on the street--put it that way. If you're
a scavenger, you're trying to survive everyday and every night. When you ask
for a job everybody says no, no, no. So you're a scavenger. Nowhere to stay,
no place to go...In the winter, the summer, whatever. It's really not funny.
It hurts. As a matter of fact I don't even want to talk about it anymore.

I know everything can't always be rosy. I don't know when or how I'll get
out of this situation. All I can do is keep my faith and strength and one day there
will be a way out. Hell doesn't last forever and this is hell. One day the Lord's
going to say that I suffered enough. Miracles do exist only if you believe.
That's why I'll be glad when I get myself a job and place to stay and I hope that I'll
never have to go through this shit no more. It hurts me, it tears me apart inside.

We've got to get him to detox soon. I'm sure you noticed that he's urinated and defecated in his pants. If you want to talk about the homeless, you have to include these things--the wine shits, the vomiting from the alcohol. It's not pleasant, but it's part of the reality.

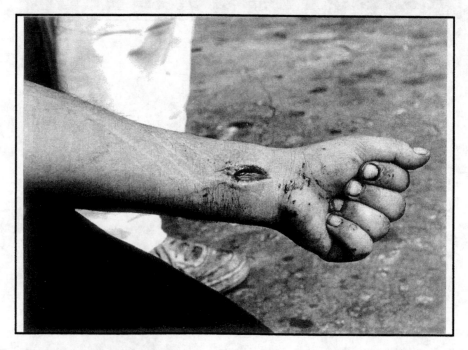

Every time he wants attention he breaks a wine bottle and cuts himself up. He'll be taken to the hospital and kept thirty or sixty days and then he'll be right back on the street.

I couldn't stay sober and stay by myself. I was too scared.

The other night a t.v. crew came by and interviewed me. I said that I don't
want them to show my face because I don't want my family to see me.
I don't want to ask my family for anything--I have my pride.

I lost my job about seven months ago. I started drinking a little too much.
I know I have a problem with it and that I'm responsible for what happens to me.
My downfall is my fault.

I don't like to ask people for money, I really don't. Someone went by
the other day and stole my cup. I don't understand why
the poor rob from the poor.

There are times when I'm in a situation that I don't want to be in like now,
but I try to smile anyway. People look at me and see the wine and they don't see
anything else. I say listen to the mind, not the wine. The intelligence is here,
but they don't want to take the time to find out.

I found some work for a while, moved out of the hotel that I was staying in.
It was bad. The rooms were as big as the size of a small car. Just room for a cot,
that's it. People were dealing drugs, shooting up. There was noise all night long
and I never knew what kinds of bugs were around. I went to another hotel
on the Bowery where there are locks on the doors. I'm trying to do better.
I go to detox sometimes but then what's the use because
I have no place to go when I get out.

Sometimes I wonder why the Lord lets me suffer so much. I think that
maybe I'm supposed to keep suffering and then He'll give me my wings
and I'll just fly up. I'm not sure that I'll even go to heaven, though.
I believe there is a heaven and hell and I'm certain that this is hell.

Don--Late 40s

The way I came to the streets of New York sounds like a bad movie.
I was living up north with my family. I went to see The Getaway with Steve
McQueen while I was high. I thought to myself "hey, I could do that.
It looks like fun." It really started as a joke. I went to a local bank with a toy
gun. I told the teller to give me all the money and she actually did.

I ran out of the bank and all of a sudden this dye bomb went off in the bag.
There was money flying all over the place. I jumped into my car and drove off.
I saved some of the money so I could give something to my daughter.

Eventually, I was caught and ended up in prison. I had done most of my
sentence but I couldn't take it anymore. This was a low security prison and it was
easy for me to escape. I hid in a laundry truck. I came to New York with a friend
of mine and figured that I wouldn't be noticed on the streets here.

On the street I got into drinking, but my body can't take it. I'm the only guy
on the street who drinks a quart of milk after a pint of wine. I've been panhandling
cars on the corner. Sometimes I can make good money but it's been dangerous
too. About a year ago I went to ask a guy in a truck for some change.
He grabbed me by the neck and said "I thought I told you to stop panhandling."
The light turned green and he drove across the street, dragging me all the way.
He stopped and smashed my head into a fire hydrant. I've been seeing a lawyer
and he keeps saying that I've got a chance at a good settlement.
He told me that it will take a few years though. His lawyer thinks
I'll just go away because I'm homeless.

I've been trying to find some work. This guy I know keeps some clothes
for me in his apartment--I have to try and look halfway decent. To look at me
now, would you think I had a B.A. in psychology and an M.A. in special ed?
It's almost impossible to have an intelligent conversation with someone when
you're on the street. I miss not being able to talk to people.

I was in the hospital for about a month with hypothermia. I couldn't even
stand up. One of the cops that knows me called an ambulance when he saw
how sick I was. The doctor said that if I had been a few degrees colder
my bodily functions would have ceased. It took two hours for my temperature
to come back to normal.

I've been going to church everyday now. The people there are great.
I've even tried to cut down on my drinking. I've been thinking about the ministry.
I'd like to help other people who have problems. I used to work with retarded
children and I'd like to do social work again. With my degree in psychology
and my experiences, I think I can do it.

Since I've cut my drinking I have much more energy. I've been writing.

"I saw a star slide down the sky
Lining the earth as it went by
Too lovely to be bothered soul
Too burning and too quick to hold
Could only to make wishes on
And then forever to be gone."

Three weeks after Don wrote this poem he was found dead from exposure to the elements.

APPENDIX

The following facilities distribute and accept clothing and is by no means complete. It is always best to call first whenever possible.

Manhattan

Bowery Mission (Men)
227 Bowery
674-3456

Epiphany Church
74 St. & York Ave.
737-2720

Goddard-Riverside/Project
        Reach-Out
593 Columbus Ave.
873-6600

Grace and Hope Mission
3rd Ave. & 14 St.
982-1230

Holy Name Center (Men)
18 Bleecker St.
226-5848

Moravian Church
30th St. & Lexington Ave.
683-4231

Olivieri Center (Women)
257 West 30 St.
947-3211

Riverside Church
122nd St. & Riverside Dr.
222-5900

St. Bartholemew's Church
109 East 50 St.
751-1616

St. John the Divine
Amsterdam Ave. & 112 St.
316-7540

Queens

Northeastern Conference of Service Center
99-13 Northern Blvd.
(718) 639-3511

Brooklyn

Angel Guardian Home/Fort Green
   Family Services
430 Myrtle Ave.
(718) 624-2100

Mount Olive House
285 Eldert St.
(718) 443-6010

Bushwick Human Services Center
144 Bleeker St.
(718) 443-5666

Most Holy Trinity Church
138 Montrose Ave.
(718) 388-3176

Bronx

Highbridge Community Life
979 Ogden Ave.
(718) 293-4352

St. John's Lutheran
1343 Fulton Ave.
(718) 293-0300

Staten Island

St. Jude Holy Coptic Orthodox
   Church
204-210 Gordon St.
(718) 448-5523

In addition, local community centers publish community service directories.
Contact your local community center for further information.